CHURCH
AND
JUSTICE
IN IGBO SOCIETY

The Relevance of Igbo Values of Justice in Igbo Christianity

(AN INTRODUCTION TO IGBO CONCEPT OF JUSTICE)

OKEY JUDE UCHE C.S.SP.

authorHOUSE®

AuthorHouse™
1663 Liberty Drive
Bloomington, IN 47403
www.authorhouse.com
Phone: 1 (800) 839-8640

Published by AuthorHouse 08/17/2017

ISBN: 978-1-5462-0157-1 (sc)
ISBN: 978-1-5462-0156-4 (e)

CONTENTS

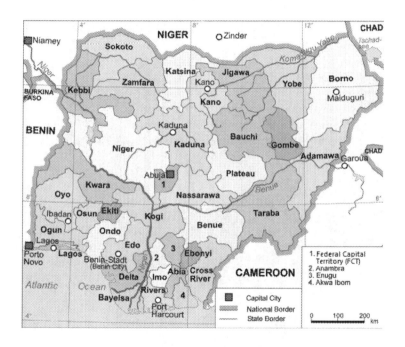

Map 1-MAP OF NIGERIA

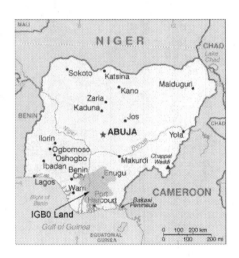

Map 2-MAP OF IGBOLAND

JUSTICE is the central star which governs society, the pole on which the political world turns, the principle and rule of all transactions. Nothing is done among men except by virtue of <u>right</u>; nothing without the invocation of justice. Justice is not the work of law at all; on the contrary, law is never anything but a declaration and application of the <u>just</u>, in all circumstances where men can find their interests related. Then if the idea that we form for ourselves of the just and of right be ill-determined, if it be incomplete or even false, it is evident, that all our legislative applications would be wicked, our institutions vicious, our politics erroneous; consequently, there would be disorder and social evil.

P.J. Proudhon
De La Justice Oeuv, IV p. 144
(trans by R.L. Hoffman: <u>Revolu-</u>
<u>tionary Justice</u>, Chicago 1972)

GENERAL INTRODUCTION

Africa is often distinguished by its close-knit societies. Customs and laws for regulating conduct and interpersonal relations are complex. A good deal has been said and written on African religion and morals, but unfortunately little or nothing has been done on the analysis of the moral and ethical attitude of Africans. Hence many scholars tend to interpret African morality only as an attitude towards cultic activities i.e. the 'Do's and 'Don't's (taboos) of the gods. Others tend to gloss over the issue arguing that African morality lacks differentiations between the ceremonial and moral aspects of law. As a result these scholars record right conduct and sin, right and wrong, good and bad, only in terms of mystical rewards and retribution.

Thus justice for these societies consists of doing "hat the gods require and, in turn, these gods ensure the survival of the society in question.

It is an indisputable fact that religion has a social importance on both individuals and societies especially in Africa, but at the same time, such importance has been stressed that, to a large extent, the African appears to be deprived of the freedom and the responsibilities of human existence.[1]

In this essay, therefore, I have chosen one African society, "the Igbos of South-east Nigeria", to investigate their philosophical concept of justice in terms of social relationships. Towards this end, I shall try to reconstruct the Igbo concept of justice by first of all inquiring

---

[1] R. Green's effort to distinguish morality from religion has greatly inspired this work. (Cf. R.M. Green: "Religion and Morality in the African Traditional Setting" Journal of Religion in Africa, vol. XIV, E.J. Brill, Leiden, 1983, pp 1-23)

into the Igbo world-view with a view to elucidating the principles of relationship which are included in justice family. The principles which have appeared as obvious values of justice are thereby examined in the light of Christian ethical values to see if they are of any relevance to Christianity in Igboland.

However, the task is not going to be easy, mainly due to the fact that studies on Igbo morality are scanty and at an early stage. Thus, anyone who is inquiring into the Igbo ethical values is likely to be confronted with the problem of distinguishing religious beliefs from ethical conduct and customs. Confronted with such a problem, I shall simply take justice to mean that inner compulsion which motivates man in his relationship with his fellow men and to God. Consequently, I shall endeavour to concern myself with justice in a social context so that it is restricted to what is generally called "social justice". Thus, the emphasis is on distributive justice and its implications rather than on legal or commutative justice.

ACKNOWLEDGMENT

I profoundly owe lots of gratitude to my mother, Ogoeto Margaret Enendu, my grandmother, Ejinwanyi and Chief Ucheawuba Osigwe who introduced me to justice and its values. They also taught me its importance in social relationships. To my uncle, Chief Sylvester Uche, who died while trying to get me ready to return to school, Holy Ghost Juniorate, Ihiala, thank you for your sacrifices. I will never forget your sufferings and will always remember you on the altar of the Most High God.

My gratitude goes to Father Peter Jeffery C.S.Sp. for accepting and moderating this essay, to my Rectors, Fathers Vincent O'Toole, Jim Brown and Brian Fulton, for their moral support.

May I also thank Marian McDonald and Mary Whitehead for typing this work. Diana Delgado occupies a special place in my heart for retyping and rearranging the whole work.

My appreciation also goes to Mr. John Harwood, the Librarian, for his tremendous help and to all who contributed to the Success of this work.

Finally, I'm highly indebted to the authors whose works I have used quite a lot in this essay. I am responsible for any inadequacies considered in this essay.

DEDICATION

*TO MY SWEET MOTHER, OGOETO MARGARET
ENENDU FOR BEING MY MOTHER WITH ALL THE
COMMITMENTS AND RESPONSIBILITIES.*

TO MAZI OZUOME ENENDU, MY STEP-FATHER, WHO
DISCOVERED SOMETHING *EXCEPTIONAL* IN ME.

OKEY J. UCHE
APRIL 2016

St. John the Baptist Church,
Baldwin Park, Ca 91706
U.S.A.

CHAPTER ONE

THE IGBO BACKGROUND

The Igbo-Who They Are And Where They Live

The aim here is not to give a detailed anthropological history of Igbo people. Instead, it is designed to give some information about the basic features of the religious, social and political institutions of the Igbos as a springboard to our study for Igbo values of justice.

However, in the present-day political structure of Nigeria, the Igbos are found in six states – Abia, Anambra, Ebony, Enugu, Imo and Delta (Bendel). In Niger Delta State, the Igbos are found on the western part of the River Niger and are referred to as Delta Igbos, in Delta state the Igbos are found on the western part of the River Niger and are referred to as Delta Igbos, and through trade and cultural links they maintain their Igbo identity.

With regard to the origin of the Igbo people, there are hardly any literary records with which to ascertain the date of origin of the Igbo. This affects not only their origin but also the means of interpreting and understanding the religious, social and political systems of the people. The only records are those based on oral tradition, myths and legends, all of which have been recorded in recent times.[2] Thus when Igbo homogeneity is examined, it becomes clear that Igbos are not Igbos because they have a common ancestry, nor are they Igbos

---

[2] Cf. E.N. Njaka: Igbo Political Culture (Northwestern Uni. Press, Evanston, 1974, pp 16-28).

because they constitute a political unit. They are rather Igbos because they have a common language and the same common language and the same cultural pattern.

Igbo Socio-Policitical Structure

The Igbo society is organized on patrilineal groups (agnatics). Since lineage determines the membership of a family group, the line of inheritance and succession to name and office, a person takes most of his jural rights in land, in social, economic and political positions from the lineage of his father. The members of his lineage are his "<u>umunna</u>" (agnates). At the same time, these segmentary lineages are bound together by the belief in the common descent from one ancestor. They had a corporate unity derived from a single lineage genealogy.

The study of political authority among the Igbo should not be confined to formal institutions. This is because there is no purely political or governmental organization and there is no clearly delineated sphere of political affairs. Hence the prevalent cliché phrase: 'Igbo *enwe eze*' (the Igbos have no kings): "which takes some significance if it is understood that in the majority of Ibo[3] territory east of the Niger, power is not centralized in the hands of a ruling monarch".[4] Western Igbo, notably Aboh, Oguta, Onitsha, Eka and Ossomari have kinship and institutions patterned on Benin and Igala. But in all, the Igbo political system is flexible, and democratic, characterized by a federation of representatives from the various lineages in elders age grades, and titled societies, which constitutes the policy-making concerned with formulating rules and standards of social behavior for the solidarity of the group as a political unit.

---

[3] In many of the early writings the orthography is "Ibo". In this work we shall maintain the original version 'Igbo" except when quoting authors. We shall use the word 'Igbo' as referring both to the people and to their language.

[4] H.O. Chukwuma: Oral Tradition of the Ibos (An unpublished Ph.D thesis in Philosophy, University of Birmingham, 1974 p. 3)

Decisions are reached by consensus. Writing about Igbo socio-political organization, Forede and Jones noted that

> "The Ibo are generally held to be
> tolerant, ultra-democratic and
> highly individualistic. They
> dislike and suspect any form of
> external government and authority."[5]

This is a way of saying that there is no dominant authority uniting all Igbos into a political unit. Thus the saying 'Igbo *enwe eze*' (Igbos have no king), though not to be taken literally (e.g. anarchy), has a more general truth in terms of socio-political consciousness and indicates clearly the hard Igbo characteristic of independence and self-assertion. In the analysis, authority among the Igbos rests with the man who has the *Ofo*[6], a symbol of truth, justice and righteousness.

Igbo Religious Beliefs And Practices

The world of the Igbo is a world of spirits. Their belief system and an elaborate religious worship organized around it confirm their assertion. "This conception of 'spirit' is deep and powerful" writes Basden, "operating from within, and is not merely an outward conformity to religious observance although it includes that. It is such a prime elemental force that it might quite fairly be described as a sixth sense as much alive, and as keenly active, as the normal five."[7]

---

[5] D.Ford of G.I. Jones: The Ibo and Ibibio Speaking Peoples of South-Eastern Nigeria, (International African Institute, London, 1960 p.24) C.f. M.M. Green: Ibo Village Affairs. (Sidwick & Jackson London 1947)

[6] "The Ofo is the central symbol of the Igbo religion. In addition to being a staff of authority, it is an emblem symbolizing the links between Chukwu and Man, the dead and the living, the living and the unborn. For these reasons, it plays many important roles in the social, political, and religious life of the Igbo." (cf. E.N.Njaka, op.cit. p.35)

[7] G.T.Basden: Niger Ibos. Frank Cass. London, (1938) 1966, p. 3.

Although Igbo religious beliefs have not been systematized into a body of dogma, the following characteristics summarize the Igbo religious beliefs. It is a tribal religion in the sense that its major tenets are shared by all Igbo-speaking people, but in matters of religious participation, it remains organisationally local; the most effective unit of religious worship is the extended family. Secondly, it is a religion of "diffused monotheism." in the sense that the Igbo worship one Supreme Being, *Chukwu* (*Chi*, God, *Ukwu*, Great) though there are intermediaries, *Ala* (earth-goddess), ancestral spirit and personal *Chi* or 'spiritual double' featuring prominently. Thirdly, the spirits (good and bad) in their numerical strength are highly competitive but yet, each still retains its sphere of independent activity and power over the living, a power which is both contractual and reciprocal. They receive sacrifices from the living and, in turn, offer them protection and prosperity.

Another important aspect of Igbo religious beliefs is the belief in Reincarnation. In this case, the influence of religion on Igbo social and moral life is tremendous because any breach of the norms regulating relationships incurs displeasure and vengeance of the gods. And as a result it could lead to the denial of reincarnation or acceptance in the land of the spirits, unless the offence is properly expiated.

Religion And Morality

With the emphasis on the existence and power of *Chukwu* and the spirits, and thus their influence on human daily life. The Igbo man very much links morality with destiny, precisely because among the Igbo people, religion, law, justice, and politics were inextricably bound and embodied in what is known as '*Omenala*'.[8] '*Omenala*' was (still is) believed to have been handed down from the spirit world, from time immemorial, from one generation to another. The gods

---

[8] '*Omenala*' means here all the practices of tradition and custom and thus forms the source of justice and moral judgments. Hence it is more often than not referred to as a moral code and this is the sense in which we shall use it in this essay.

are very important in sanctioning and reinforcing this moral code. They are therefore the custodians of the religious, legal and moral practices of the Igbo people; prominent among these gods is the earth-goddess, *Ala*. She is the unseen president of the small localised community gods. And, of course, no Igbo community is complete without a shrine of *Ala* (the earth-goddess). Consequently in matters of morality, *Chukwu* is rarely the focal point. Moreover, he is, for the Igbo, so good and merciful that he rarely punishes anybody who daily strives to be just in all his conduct.

Fears of punishment and shame are more public-orientated than for individual relationship with God. Ritual sacrifice is therefore geared towards restoring social relations and the harmony that exists between the parties involved.

The Igbo religious beliefs and socio-political institutions thus played an important part in upholding standards of behaviour so vital to stability and peace in an Igbo community. This is the basis of Igbo ontological existence.

⊷ ⊷

CHAPTER TWO

THE PRINCIPLES OF JUSTICE IN TRADITIONAL IGBO SOCIETY

Introduction

U ntil recently Western scholars have failed to appreciate the extent to which the African way of life is founded upon a system of anthropology and ethics. Consequently much attention has been focused on myths, gods and rituals, but these are far from being the sum total and substance of African socio-religious life. They are only partial ingredients within a total view at the centre of which lies a moral conception of man and all his environs. This conception is a complex one and involves notions of personal identity, freedom, destiny, god, ancestors and social ethics.

It is pertinent here, therefore, that to get a proper understanding of our topic we shall try to analyse how the Igbos evaluate life by focusing our attention on the cosmology of the Igbo. This cosmology would explain, for the Igbo, how everything came into being – the origin of God and the Spirits, the origin of the world, the meaning

---

[9] The solutions of Greek philosophy to the problem "of change in being remain purely intellectual. Except indirectly and incidentally, they have no value dimension in which emotions and the will would play a part. Indeed the self-determination of the free will, which is an essential part of any ethical system based on metaphysical principles, remains one of the most mysterious and unsatisfactory chapters even among the best of Aristotlian philosphers. (cf. E.A. Ruch and K.C. Anyanwu: African Philosophy, Catholic Book Agency, Rome, 1981, p. 144 ff.)

of life, the origin of man and destiny. It also provides them with an 'action-system', i.e. the principles guiding human behaviour. It is this second aspect that will be our concern later in this study since it is within it that one finds the principles of justice which lie in the series of relationships between man and the universe and which are perceived in terms of life-forces. No doubt this applies to most societies which have built many of their social, moral and legal structures on ancestor-worship and the extended family.[10]

The Igbo World-View-A World Of Hierarchical Forces

The creation of the universe is believed to be the work of *Chineke*,[11] God, the Creator. According to Igbo myths, *Chineke* created two worlds, a world of man full of animate and inanimate beings and a world of spirits. The spirit world is the abode of *Chineke*, also known as *Chukwu*, the spirits, and the ancestors. Man, though he comes from the spirit world[12], has no immediate access to it until he dies.

These myths expound very strongly the constant interaction between the two worlds of man and spirit. And this is highlighted by the dominating power of *Chukwu* who manifests himself in everyone and in everything in the universe.[13] In this way, the world for the Igbo is primarily a community of beings, with god as the head. And

---

[10] V.C. Uchendu: The Igbo of South-east Nigeria (Holt, Rinehart and Winston, N.Y., London, 1965 p. 11)

[11] God as the Supreme Being is also addressed in so many other names in Igboland, such as 'Chukwu' (the supreme Being), 'Osebuluwa' (he who upholds the world), etc. (cf. LA. Arinze: Sacrifice in Igbo Religion, Ibadan, University Press, 1970, pp 10-12)

[12] It is the Igbo metaphysical view of the human personality that when a man dies he is reborn into the world-the Igbo doctrine of Reincarnation. (cf. C.K. Meek: Law and Authority in a Nigerian Tribe, OXFORD University Press, London, 1937, pp 53-54 f; cf also V.C. Uchendu, op. cit.p. 13)

[13] "Being" in Igbo metaphysical thought is inseparably attached to "life-force". (cf. E. Metuh: God and Man in African Religion. Geoffrey Chapman, London, 1981, pp. 48-59, ff. esp. P. Tempels' Bantu Philosophy, (collection *Presnece Africaine* (English Edition) Paris, 1959, pp.30-39).

so whatever any member of this community does, whether he is a man or spirit, animate or inanimate, it invariably affects the entire community, with God foreseeing an controlling the entire universe. This is what constitutes the Igbo theory of life-force.

Moreover, the Igbo world-view sees both the material and spiritual worlds as stages of existence accessible to man's vital force. Existence, for the Igbo, is therefore a dualistic and inter-related phenomenon involving the interaction between the material and spiritual. This is the core and theory of Reincarnation.[14] Thus what most scholars regard as the anthropomorphic attitude of the Igbos is nothing but the refusal of the Igbo cultural spirit to give a separate and static existence to abstract notions, notions which obscure the relationships between the world of man and the world of the spirit.

The relationship between the two worlds constitutes for the Igbo an essential order and character of the universe as a whole. In the words of Tempels, it is "an intimate ontological relationship...comparable with the causal tie which binds creature and creator".[15] This however does not mean that the Igbo do not make any distinctions between the two worlds; on the contrary, the Igbo accord recognition to the mode of operation of the life-forces in both worlds. The same distinction is made between the animate and inanimate beings. It is the Igbo belief that the difference in the natural endowment of life-force also determines to a large extent the sort of relationship existing between each and every other being. With the uniqueness of each life-force, beings, spiritual and material alike can influence, reinforce or weaken one or the other.

This theory of life-force explains why the Igbo regard some creatures as having extraordinary powers influencing some to do good for the sake of others, and others to become anti-social, practising witchcraft, sorcery, jealousies, greed, and so on. It is very

---

[14] Uchendu, op. cit. p. 13. Uchendu gave a detailed account of the Igbo concept of life after death. It is worth noting the Igbo sense of reward and punishment is the motivating idea for the quest for an irreproachable life and has much to do with their concept of justice.

[15] Tempels, op. cit. p.40

important to realise that among the Igbos, this extraordinary power could be spiritual or material. It is spiritual when it is interpreted as the will of *Chukwu*, for instance, the power to foresee what would happen in the future could only be seen by the Igbo as a revelation. And it is material when it is interpreted as evil: for example, when a man becomes a sorcerer or wizard.[16] Hence there was little or no effort in Igbo traditional society to distinguish between physical and spiritual realities. All things have not only their origin in God, but they are different as well.

In other words, God, spirit, man, ancestors, and indeed the universe, are all living forces though they belong to different levels of the hierarchy of forces and whose unity can only be seen in the context of social relationships. The notion of hierarchical forces in Igbo world-view connotes the principle of seniority which in turn ensures stability and continuity in the social order of the universe.

Maintaining The Ontological Balance

At the first glance of the Igbo world view, one might quickly conclude that the natural order goes on its ordained way according to a 'master plan', but such would be a misunderstanding of Igbo cosmological ideas. In reality the Igbo world is a dynamic one, a world of moving equilibrium. It is an equilibrium that is constantly threatened, and sometimes actually disturbed by natural disasters like long, continuous famine, shortage of rain, epidemic disasters as well as sorcery, witchcraft and other anti-social forces, such as litigation, homicide, violations of community laws (taboos), and are thus defined as *Aru* (abomination or pollution).

To avert these calamities, therefore, the Igbos believe that the ontological order of the universe can be maintained through certain

---

[16] The concept of god in Igbo thought exists side by side with the notion of devil. The most important difference between the two notions is that devil is subjected to God, but He allows him enormous power to carry out diabolic actions in man. Hence devil is sometimes personified in a vaguely characterised being, 'Ekwensu'.

principles which would create an atmosphere where every being, man or spirit, can together develop its respective personality and work out its destiny as well. These principles make up what is known as *"Omenala"* (code of behaviour and customs).

Omenala is believed, according to Igbo myths, to have been handed over to the Igbos orally by the Earth-goddess (*Ala*) through the ancestors. This Earth-goddess also sees to the maintenance and enforcement of *Omenala* through her priests, heads of various extended families and, above all, through the various local (village and town) councils.

Ala is regarded as the owner of men, whether alive or dead. The cult of ancestors is, therefore, closely associated with that of the *Ala* who is the Queen of the underworld. She is the fount of human morality, and is, as a result, a principal legal and moral sanction. Homicide, kidnapping, poisoning, stealing, adultery, giving birth to twins or abnormal children, and so on, are all offences against *Ala* which must be purged through ritual sacrifices to her. Hence it is the Igbo belief that *Ala* deprives evil men of their lives and wealth. Her priests are the guardians of public morality. Laws are therefore made and enforced in her name and by her oaths are sworn. She is the mainspring of social life, and, in many localities, if anyone wishes to better his social position by taking titles, then he must first secure the blessings of *Ala*. She is, indeed, the unseen leader of every community, and no group is complete without a shrine of *Ala*. Above all, every action is always under her scrutiny.[17]

For the Igbo, therefore, existence is conceived in terms of interaction and exchange of forces, all of which ultimately share in the fundamental force of the Creator whose super abundance of force manifested itself in its fullness at the moment of creation. Hence the *Omenala* (lit. the "doings" or "ways" of the "land") is essentially a working principle, or moral code, which directs individuals and

---

[17] The common possession of a shrine of Ala is one of the strongest integrating forces in Igbo society

groups towards the realization of (what is now an obligation) this ontological character of creation.[18]

The basic rule underlying the Igbo *Omenala* seems to be: what is "natural" is right; What is "unnatural" is wrong. Thus incest is not natural for it contravenes the 'natural pattern of human behaviour and exposes man and his group to divine retribution. Adultery is also not natural because it unjustly deprives the other man of his right. Consequently, the most immediately felt aspect of the order of nature and the one which most intimately and continuously affect Igboman's life is the social order as lived in his family, village and town.

In the mythical worldview of the Igbo there is no such thing as an individual being, totally distinct and totally separable from other beings. And since all "beings are ultimately related to a a common creator as a central source of force and of being, all entities are related to each other and are ontologically connected with each other at a much deeper level of their being".[19]

Existence is therefore conceived as an interaction and exchange of forces, all of which ultimately share in the fundamental force of the Creator. Thus the Igbo conception of the universe is essentially religious.

The Social Concept Of Man In Igboland

The Igbo concept of man is simple though it is not systematically thought out as in the Western philosophy. However, for our better understanding of the Igbo concept of man, it is good to observe that in Igbo thought, man does not have a split personality: "he is an organic whole."[20] All his parts, the body, the heart, the spirit, and so on, form a unity which responds together to the source of its being. Man for the Igbo is simply a creature of *Chukwu* who ultimately determines his destiny. God has put i n to man, the Igbo believe,

---

[18] E. Ilogu: <u>Christianity and Igbo Culture</u>, (Nok publ. London, 1974, pp. 123-128)

[19] E.A. Ruch & K. C. Anyanwu, op. cit. pp. 149-151

[20] J.S. Pobee (ed): Religion, Morality and Population Dynamics, (Uni. of Ghana, Legon, 1977, p. 70)

an inner capacity for reason, freedom, and above all, the sense of morality. Even man's ignorance does not excuse him from keeping the social ontological order of his environment. Thus, morality is immediately linked to destiny and manmade morally acceptable.

The traditional belief is that man is an encapsulated spirit and not an animated body, a character which differentiates man from mere animal. Hence it is high offensive and totally reprehensible to call man an animal (*anu-ohia*) among the Igbos.

The complexity of the Igbo concept of man is further exemplified by the Igbo belief that each individual is endowed with a spiritual affinity known as "*Chi*" at the very moment of his conception. This chi is a kind of spiritual double, linking man to God, his ancestors and the unborn. He is, in short, the means of communion with the spirit world. *Chi* is therefore charged with the responsibility of guiding and protecting the individual during his life-time and leaves him at death to continue his full existence in the spiritual world. He is morally and socially responsible for man's behaviour throughout his life on earth.

Chi, as it were, represents individual freedom, responsibility, fortunes, and destiny in a person. Meek calls it a "personal genius,"[21] similar to the creative intelligence of God. A man's abilities, faults, and good or bad fortunes are ascribed to his *Chi*, and this explains, to some extent the fatalistic attitude of the Igbo and consequently affects a long range of actions which are part and parcel of everyday life. For example, if an Igbo man gets into trouble, he blames everything on his *Chi*. Everybody, therefore, wants to be in harmony with his *Chi* so that it will always help him in his life. The Igbo negotiates with *Chukwu* (*Chi-Ukwu*), the Supreme Being, through *Ala* and other gods, but he deals directly with his *Chi*, his ancestors, other men, and indeed with everything or anyone he encounters. "Manipulation and negotiations are", for the Igboman, "ways of getting ahead in life, because of the Igbo belief that life is like a market".[22]

---

[21] C.K. Meek, op. cit. p. 55
[22] E. Njaka, op. cit., pp. 31-33

Precisely because man's chi helps to define his personality and helps him to define his relationships with other people around whom he sees as having the same life-force and mission as himself. As indeed Nowell-Smith rightly noted:

> "Growing up morally is learning to
> cope with the world into which we
> find ourselves pitched, and especially
> to cope with our relations with other
> human beings".[23]

A person is, therefore, in Igbo thought, considered first and foremost as a constituent of a particular community, "for it is the community which defines who he is and who he can become".[24] Mbiti aptly puts it thus: "the individual is conscious of himself in terms of 'I am because we are, and since we are, therefore I am".[25] That is, the Igbo recognise every individual person as a unique person endowed by the Creator with his own personality and talents, and motivated by his own particular needs and ambitions. But at the same time, in Igbo socio-political system (institutions), there are various checks and balances on personal rights and freedom in relation to the total social and historical context.

The Igbo socio-political structures never approximate the western notion of individualism, namely the idea that men could be independent of their social and historical circumstances. The Igbo world view is, in a way, too systematic for such a doctrine. It is also logically and dynamically integrated.

In other words, "freedom and individuality" in Igbo traditional

---

[23] I.T. Ramsey (ed.): <u>Christian Ethics and Contemporary Philosophy</u>, (S.C.M. Press, London, 1966, p.98). In this work the author also gave a good treatment of moral socialization in societies.

[24] B.C. Ray: <u>African Religion: Symbol, Ritual and Community</u>, (Prentice-Hall, Inc., Englewood Cliffs, New Jersey, 1965, p.132).

[25] J. Mbiti: <u>African Religions and Philosophy</u>, (Heinemann, London 1969, pp.92-109).

society, "are always balanced by destiny and community, and these are in turn balanced by natural and supernatural powers. Every person is a nexus of interacting elements of the self and of the world which shape and is shaped by his behavior".[26] Thus life in the Igbo world is founded on interaction and most importantly on reciprocity. Both the interests of an individual and of the community are to a large extent interwoven.

The interests of the community are assured when the individual acts in concern with the community i.e. acts in compliance with the values of the community. The community in turn gives moral and concrete support which assures continued protection of the individual interests as a person-in-community. But to achieve this balance, like any other human endeavour, is never totally successful.

This struggle to balance social relations represents the tension in the Igbo social life between what is "natural" and what is "unnatural"; what is "right" and what is "wrong". Consequently, what is natural in most primal societies is always taken as "right", the ideal, and the "unnatural" as "wrong" and thus to be avoided. Such unnatural phenomena hinder the fullness of life and restoration is only possible by ritual sacrifices through which social relationships are renewed.

In the case of the Igbos, the ideal social relations and interaction is reflected in the various ways in which they have practiced and preserved justice in their tradition. This is the relevance of their concepts of God, man and community in their world-view, for it is in the mutual relationships existing between them that the Igbo base their concept of total social harmony as an ideal.

---

[26] B, C, Ray, op, cit. p, 132

CHAPTER THREE

CONCEPT OF JUSTICE IN THE IGBO TRADITIONAL SOCIETY

Introduction

In this section we shall try to re-construct the Igbo concept of justice and proceed to consider justice in Igbo society as a moral quality in relationships. Given the Igbo world-view of action as already discussed, it then becomes necessary to show how the interactions and relationships in the universe relate to the Igbo –traditional concept of justice. As we have already noted, the rightness and wrongness of action is, in general, determined by the goodness or badness of their consequences. This sort of notion is common to most cultures. The question to be addressed now is the Igbo concept of justice.

Justice

It is important, however, that before we proceed to re-construct the concept of justice in Igbo traditional Society, we try to give in brief a general view of the concept of justice in both the Graeco-Roman and Judeo-Christian milieu.

In the Graeco-Roman tradition "justice is seen primarily as that which orders man's relations to his fellows and which inspires the laws that guarantee the equilibrium and the tranquility of the community".[27] When the Greek philosophers attributed this absolute primacy to justice they were implying the term in its more general sense as a principle of harmony in the community. Plato, for example, sees a just man as one who performs the task or function proper to him in accordance with his place in society. For Aristotle, justice connotes conformity with law because this produces and preserves the happiness of the community, and thus a just man is the law-abiding man.[28]

In Judaeo-Christian tradition, one encounters an even wider concept of justice. Firstly, "there is the justice of God as the intrinsic harmony of the divine will. Corresponding to this justice of God there is a justice of man. It denotes holiness or action in conformity with the divine will, whether or not one's action has relation to other persons".[29]

Within these two traditions, one can already see the difficulties involved in the use of this term "justice", and such apparent lack of a clear-cut definition often conceals or distorts the meaning of justice. However, within this general concept of justice, one can still deduce a more technical concept which presupposes "otherness" and thus could be taken as 'rendering to each his due'. The theoretical rigor of these traditional presuppositions in the final analysis result in the classical division of justice: individual or commutative justice, social and distributive justice.[30]

What of the Igbo tradition, what is its concept of justice? And does this concept constitute any moral value in Igbo morality?[31]

---

[27] E. McDonagh (ed.): <u>Moral Theology Renewed</u>, (Gill and Son, Dublin, 1965, p. 152)

[28] T. Campbell: <u>Seven Theories of Human Society</u>, (Clarendon Press, Oxford, 1981, p. 56-59)

[29] E. McDonagh, op. ci. p. 153

[30] Daniel Maguire: <u>A New American Justice</u>, (Winston Press, U.S.A. 1980, p. 65)

[31] I shall be relying highly on the classical vocabulary in re-constructing the Igbo notion of justice.

Justice As Moral Rectitude[32]

Moral philosophers have maintained that every society has various ways of characterizing what is good and bad; true and false; just and unjust. This applies too to the Igbo. The question of physical and moral good and evil is so elementary to the Igbo that one would be astonished in his attempt to uncover the coherence of justice within itself as an idea and within social reality.

In the Igbo world-view we saw God as the first in the hierarchical order of beings and, above all, as the source of life-force. Within this Igbo concept of God, one finds that for the Igbo, god is all-powerful and lord over all inferior spirits. He is generous in his favours to mankind. Consequently, he is conceived as the upholder of social order, the source and sanction of public justice. Thus justice in Igbo thought rests fundamentally on the character and will of God, *Chukwu,* who established the social order of the universe. His justice, therefore, lies in his will and power to maintain the harmonious order of the world and in the will he punishes those who act contrary to the norms regulating this ontological social order.

In this respect the Igbo thought is very similar to the Judaeo-Christian tradition. Hence, in biblical thought, justice *(mishpat)* is seen specifically as the righteousness *(tsedeq)* of God.[33]

Justice was, in Igbo language, a moral value. It appears frequently in synonymous relation with "righteousness". "Righteousness is a quality of intention and act, a characteristic of persons" and from thence it flows out into interpersonal relations, and, ultimately terminates in a quality of the community itself.

To express this concept the Igbo' use *Ikwubakaoto*. Etymologically

---

[32] The word 'moral rectitude' *is* used here in relation to justice to express the harmony within a person which comes from a right relationship between the person and his environment.

[33] New Catholic Encyclopaedia, Vol VIII (McGraw-Hill Book, London, 1967, p. 73). It. sees love, justice, mercy, as characterizing the divine nature.

[34] J.L. Mays: IIJustice: Perspective from t he Prophetic Tradition", Interpretation, Vol. 17, 1983, p. 8.

'*Aka*' which means <u>hand</u> represents the whole person is suffixed to *nkwumoto*, meaning straightness. To say that something is straight (*kwuoto*) in a physical sense means lack of curve or crookedness. *Nkwumoto* can also refer to a subject in a sentence to describe the action of such a subject. For example, *Ikwumoto amalugo Obi ahu'* (standing has become a part of Obi's life). Thus when the Igbo use *nkwumoto* to describe somebody, then it is not just a physical description; the moral character of the individual is what is now under consideration. In other words, *ikwubakaoto* in this sense is more than mere physical straightness: it is a moral straightness.

It is a moral quality which presupposes an attitude of love, peace, justice, integrity and, above all, self-regulation. The individual is righteous. All these elements give rise to inner harmony, consequently manifested in external actions of the individual as opposed to struggle, tensions and conflicts between the self and his external action.

In another sense *ikwubakaoto* (keeping hand straight) metaphorically refers to a person who is even-handed and considerate in his transactions with others. Justice in this sense means fairness, an attitude seeking to a friendship,[35] a harmonious relationship between persons. Hence much has been said in favour of the fact that justice is held to be normative for the relation between individuals and communities.[36] Justice as a moral quality is therefore present when a person tries to fulfill the possibilities of given or assumed relationships in a way that is fair and favourable to others.

"To do justice", says Mays, "is to love good, to prefer that which makes for life. It is to hate evil, to avoid that which diminishes life".[37] Thus the Igbo man seeking harmony between himself and his environment, not only seeks the correlates of justice such as truth, love, integrity for the purpose of good life, but also seeks to

---

[35] 'Friendship' though it has a very broad meaning, is used here to describe the relationship of persons who are close to one another. As a basic purpose of good, however, friendship encompasses many other things-e.g. justice, love and peace among individuals and groups.

[36] G. Grisez and R. Shaw, op. cit. pp. 67 – 70

[37] J. Mays, op. cit. p. 11

respect other persons around as a way to realize the good life. And for the Igbo, good life here includes long and prosperous life, many children, many titles, good death and elaborate funeral ceremonies and reincarnation after death. These are what every Igbo man seeks in life. This is the value of justice: that harmonious relationship and mutual respect for another and which is *sine qua non* for life. This is what O'Donnell meant when he said: "the Ibo have a strong sense of justice, and are keen to sense your friendly or unfriendly attitude towards them".[38] Hence for Kelbley, justice's

> "...primary role is to specify the
> conditions under which personal
> harmony may be attained. It always
> seeks to disclose the factual circumstances
> which ground personal harmony. In its
> capacity, justice aims at the widest
> possible understanding of human being, both
> in its frailty and in its strength"[39]

Thus justice for the Igbo is not just a mere moral value but cannot be separated from existence because its absence is regarded as disclosing a radical flaw in the whole character of a person or an institution. In Igbo tradition, therefore, justice is seen as an attitude inherent in man and reinforcible by the sanction of *Chukwu* and other gods as part of the social order of the universe.

Justice As Judgment

This notion follows necessarily from what we have seen already. Here justice as judgment represents that situation or state of affairs which is frequently referred to as something which "ought" to be as

---

[38] W.E. Donnell: "Religion and Morality Among the Ibo of Southern Nigeria". Primitive Man, 44 (1931) p. 57

[39] C. Kelbley (ed.): The Value of Justice, Winston Press, U.S.A. 1980. P. 60

opposed to that which "ought not" to be. This is judgment, an attitude which recognizes an act as good or bad, just or unjust, depending on whether what is done has any relation with that which "ought" to be. That is, acts are judged good or bad, just or unjust if they conform to the publicity accepted standards of actions.

It is less surprising that in Igbo traditions, *'Onye n'akwuba aka ya oto'* (a person who keeps his hand straight) is one who conforms to the law (*Omenala*)[40]. And as Aristotle noted, such conduct 'produces and preserves the happiness of the community'.

Justice too, is usually referred to leaders who pronounce judgements while presiding over disputes. As it were, they hold the "mean" between law and lawlessness. Quoting Nzomiwu, Dine holds that "*Ikpe nkwumoto* (just judgment) refers specially to justice in judgments. *Ikpe* judgment) *nkwumoto* (straightness) therefore literally means judgment that stands straight, without any crookedness whatever or any quibbling to evade the truth involved is an issue".[41] This is in line with Pritchard's remarks that "the obligation to speak the truth ... involves a relation consisting of the fact that others are trusting us to speak the truth ... a relation the apprehension of which gives rise to the sense that communication of the truth is something owing by us to them".[42]

Evading truth in judgment is equal to the destruction of justice and consequently risking life itself. It is worth remembering that in the Igbo world-view, life is guaranteed by observing and maintaining "the moral character and the ontological structure of the universe".[43]

Otherwise it would mean the negation of the life-force which

---

[40] The laws prescribe about all manner of things aiming at the common interest of all ... and so in one sense we apply the term just to whatever tends to produce and preserve the happiness ·of the community' (cf The Ethics of Aristotle (Trans. by I.A.K. Thomson, Penguin Books, Baltimore, 153, Nic. Ethics, 5, 1, 13)

[41] G.U. Dine: <u>Traditional Leadership as Service Among the Igbo of Nigeria</u>, (Pontifical Uni Lateraenense, Rome, 1983, pp. 86-87)

[42] A.I. Melden: <u>Rights and Persons</u>, (Basil Blackwell, Oxford, London 1977, pp. 59-60)

[43] E.E. Uzukwu: "Igbo Spirituality as Revealed Through Igbo Prayers" <u>L'Afrique et Ses Formes De Vie Spirituelle</u>, vol. 17, 1983, p. 167

would automatically invoke the wrath of *Chukwu, onye n'ekpesara o bie'* (God the supreme Judge) and who, together with the other spirits, especially Ala, are the upholders of social order. The Igbo look upon their leaders as God's delegates who are therefore expected in all their actions to show the same impartiality which God would show in dealing with His people. In other words, they are expected to exhibit a high standard of justice. They are also expected to deal with petitioners in accordance with the law and equity and help them to their rights especially when it concerns the weak and oppressed.

Ikwubakaoto is here a very important and supreme value. For acting on the contrary could lead to death and punishments.

No wonder the Igbo hold that *"eziokwu bu ndu"* (truth is life). And of course, not everybody can be a leader in Igboland[44] and those who happen to move into such a position of leadership are expected to possess the traditional value of justice which obliges a judge, especially with the *ofo* as symbol of justice, to pronounce 'Ikpe Nkwumoto'. He must uphold justice at all costs, because the survival of the people and tradition depends on this. Thus, this brings out the fact that justice is an indispensable value among the Igbo in general and the leaders in particular.

In the Igbo view, therefore, justice is a reality as that which assigns each his due, grounding his relationship in all transactions and associations, and holding balance in social relations. All are submerged in corporate and mutual existence. For the Igbo therefore, it is possible to act justly in the courts and in the economy as a necessary consequences of man's personality and individuality as well as of the social order of the world.

---

[44] It is significant to note that the indigenous Sources of justice and judgment among the Igbo, and kin groupings reflect the highly segmented character of their society and the number of independent sources of influence and authority (cf. H. Kuper and L. Kuper (eds) African Law: Adaptation and Development, Uni. of Calif. Press, Berkeley & Los Angeles, 1955, pp 79-97)

The Communal Justice

The justice with which we are concerned here, is society, a moral quality of human relations and structures as they cohere to form the Igbo traditional society. The aim here is to show as much as possible, given a historical and cultural context, it is possible to assert that Igbo society practised social justice, perhaps, in a way peculiar to them following what we have seen in Igbo concept of justice. To this effect, we shall concern ourselves with the analysis of the criteria which the Igbo apply in distributing socially those benefits and burdens to which no particular person had a prior claim or responsibility.

The "thing" to be distributed in this connection does not include land, since under the Igbo "land tenure"[45] and as primary agriculturists, no member of the lineage is without land.

However, in discussing social justice in Igbo land one thing one needs to be clear about is the traditional Igbo view of life which emphasises above all else the human individuality and interdependence. Thus, starting from the basic social unit, the family, to the highest socio-political organisations, life is conceived of and interpreted in terms of sharing. It's a precious value that binds people and families together. It is a value that enables people to have a common understanding, leading them to mutual trust, help, respect for personal freedom, as well as mutual responsibility. In other words, life as experienced in an Igbo community is one that calls for constant inter-action and inter-relationships of people working for the benefit of all, co-operating with one another in meeting the basic necessities of life. One only needs to read some of the numerous materials on African way of life.

It is within this shared community-life that one could discover most principles of the justice family explicitly expressed in other societies. There may be aberrations, but as Aristotle rightly noted: "We apply the term "justice" to whatever tends to produce and preserve the

---

[45] C.K. Meek, op. cit. pp. 100-104. the difference he made between an individual and lineage holding is most striking.

happiness of the community".[46] It is in this context that one can really interpret the various forms of justice: commutative, general justice, and distributive, according to the Aristotelian-Thomist concepts of justice.

Thus in the classical notion of ownership, it is something which implies an absolute and exclusive right to the object by an individual within the legal norms including the right to use and to dispose of it as one wishes.[47] In Igbo society, ownership is rarely of this kind. Within the Igbo system distinctions have to be made between those things which the individual holds exclusive and unconditional rights such as farming tools and clothes, and those which the individual holds under certain conditions such as land or even cattle. Land, for example, is based on kinship and controlled by the senior member of the lineage.

However, from whatever angle one would see the notion of ownership in Igbo land, what is clear is that particular individual right to anything is in essence the rights of his (extended) family. It is therefore "family property which matters, both to the family as such and to the individuals in the family. And because it is family property all members have an equal right to a share in its use, and all have a right to participate in the process of sharing".[48]

The idea of sharing is thus basic to the notion of social justice and consequently necessary for a harmonious relationship among the individuals of any community. In *Pacem in Terris* Pope John XXIII lays down the principle:

---

[46] Nicomachen Ethics, op. cit. 5, I, 13
[47] Cf. David Miller: Social Justice, (Clarendon Press, Oxford, 1976 pp. 259 and pp. 286-299)
[48] J.W. Sempebwa: "African Traditional Moral Norms and Their Implications for Christianity, (The Steyl Press, Netherlands, 1983, pp 122-130)

"Every human being is a person, his
nature is endowed with intelligence
and free-will. By virtue of this
he has rights and duties, flowing
directly and simultaneously from
his very nature, which are "therefore
universal, inviolable and inalienable."[49]

The system of ownership or rights in Igbo society clearly recognizes the moral responsibilities involved as a result of the kind of the membership of the community. As we said earlier, the Igbo community is a community characterized by shared commitment on the part of its members to the realisation of some fundamental human purposes and by structures and activity appropriate to bringing this about. And within this context the judgment of justice is usually made.

The members may not get an equal share in the goods available, but they all have equal right to their share. There is no question of one person taking what he wants, and the rest having what is left over; every consideration, indeed moral consideration, is taken to ensure that whatever fact that makes them equal, e.g. strength, merit, status is stressed and that which makes them unequal, say physical or mental disability is also stressed. This illustrates the attitude of the Igbo towards material goods or economy of goods, contrary to the Hobbian world of "jungle" in which social relations and the Society are means of achieving selfish-interests.

Hobbes, conceives justice as an arbiter restraining men from doing harm to the other and assures them of their benefits they wish for themselves.[50]

The Igbo hold the opposite view; benefit is not the essence of life.

---

[49] C.T.S. London 1963, p. 9

[50] Hobbes analysis of human nature appears to make peaceful and co-operative human relationships impossible. He never in constructing his 'social contract' envisage men as social beings but rather as atomised individuals free to contract and disintegrate relationships and society. (cf. T. Campbell op. cit. pp 73-79)

Its economic theory therefore is that there is an abundance of goods and no man is in control of these goods except *Chukwu* (God) but in his generosity has given man power to accumulate as much as he can for his benefit and the well-being of kinsmen.[51] But acquiring as much goods as one wishes is impossible except through co-operation of one's neighbour. And according to the Igbo belief values, everybody has not been endowed with the same personality and destiny. Therefore no man is in competition with another in the negative sense as used by Hobbes. Instead of fighting to attain to economic goals, men must help each other because, according to the proverb: *'Udele erighi rna ozu anwughi'* (The vulture does not eat except where there is carcass). In other words, no man attains a position, however prominent, except with the help of his brothers. The Igbo go further than this by saying that even in a situation where the goods are scarce, people must share with each other. This idea is contained in the Igbo proverb: *Ogu Ugali onwa ano bu onu nratu n'atu* (the time of the famine is sustained by sharing the little you have).

Thus sharing is an important notion in the Igbo attitude to the economy of goods. As Nyere points out, "it was the right of sharing which served to maintain and strengthen the social unit and make it worthwhile to all its members, so there was a corresponding common duty. Every member of the social unit had the obligation to contribute to the pool of things to be shared ..••.,,[52] But that does not mean that all must contribute equally, though equality is the ideal.

Therefore the notion of sharing work to produce goods, and the notion of sharing the produced goods go hand-in-hand in Igbo thought. As a result these two notions constitute moral obligations: firstly, no one individual can accumulate wealth at the expense of others despite his freedom to do so. Secondly, the nature of the community obliges individual to practice "distributive justice as a virtue by accepting uncomplainingly the just distribution of burdens

---

[51] Compare Gen 9:1 – 3
[52] J.W. Sempebwa op. cit p. 129

and privileges without making immoderate or excessive claims against the community".[53]

This once again illustrates the fact that every form of justice is included in and presupposed by social justice, but in the latter case it is always a question of rights and duties that derive from the nature of human community and of the person. Transactions are not primary. It is rather the social nature of man that is primary, the encompassing social purpose of all earthly goods, and also the abilities of the person. That is, whatever right individuals may hold, there is a corresponding obligation in justice: "To one man's right there corresponds a duty in all other persons; the duty namely of acknowledging and respecting the right in question" (*Pacem in Terris*, p. 15). This is the law of reciprocity, of mutual dependence.

Thus the most valuable general definition of justice seems to be "that which brings out its distributive character most plainly: justice is *suum cuique*, to each his due".[54] Consequently, social justice is that in which each individual has exactly those benefits and burdens which are due to him by virtue of his personal characteristics and circumstances.

Therefore, social and distributive justice in the Igbo concept not only includes other aspects of justice, but it emphasizes the oneness of justice and thus becomes a springboard for the other values that make life worth living *iri* a social setting.

The tension arising from the duties of justice is further demonstrated by the Igbo philosophy of "live-and-let-live"[55] a maxim which has become a watchdog among the Igbos against over-individualistic tendencies and emphasizes the demand for altruism in social relationships. Thus, in the Igbo tradition, the principles of socio-distributive justice states with how the good is to be divided (say, on equal basis), or it may specify some property of the individual

---

[53] Bernard Haring: The Law of Christ, (trans. by E.G. Kaiser, The Mercier Press, Cork, 1967 p. 26)

[54] D. Miller, op. cit. p.20

[55] Chinua Achebe: Things Fall Apart, (Heinemann Press, London 1958, pp 17-18)

which will determine his share including the allocation according to needs, all for the realisation of communal solidarity.

In this sense justice is a supreme moral value for the Igbo.

Social Distribution Of 'Acquired Goods' And Burdens

The goods which we have chosen to refer to here as 'acquired goods' include those goods which are obtained through joint effort The Igbo distribution of such goods is based on the criteria of "to each according to the value of his skill and services", a criterion very much similar to that of Aristotle.

The proverb *"onye lukaria orikaria'* (he who works hard is rewarded accordingly) describes the fundamental principles of Igbo distributive justice. Its essence is that it enables members of the community as incentives to contribute selflessly to the common good. Again, the individual and the community are portrayed as two social entities. This is illustrated by animal carcass after hunting. Usually the carcass is divided according to the part played by the hunter in the hunt.

In socio-distribution of 'acquired goods', there are many different grounds considered by the Igbo for a just allotment of benefits. Some of these grounds are wholly vague, others are not, and may not be guided by the principles of justice. The principle of just distribution of benefits has always stated thus: "To be just or unjust, one must be guided by reasons of some sort. One must take each person seriously and consider whether the solution is one acceptable to him".[56] The question of share-size, therefore, is made with reference to reasons which take into account the individuality of the person governed by his circumstances.

The principles that feature prominently in the equitable social. distribution of acquired goods as is the case in the classical Aristotelian-Thomist tradition include need, status, entitlement and desert. How much weight should be given these criteria in Igbo society depends partly on the nature of the good and partly on the purpose of

---

[56] J.R. Lucas: On Justice (Clarendon Press, London, 1980, p. 164)

the associations that has be disposal of the good in question.[57] These principles and their distinctions are more often than not taken for granted and are never questioned.

To the Igbo himself, however, the concepts of need, status, merit, and entitlement are evidently clear for he uses relevant models to distinguish one principle from another. Two examples will illustrate our point.

In the wealth-prestige model, the Igbo always show the various distinctions between wealth (*aku/ uba*), status (*okwa*) and prestige (*odo*). These stress wealth and prestige in "status placement"[58] in the society. This model aims at emphasising the individual skill, his freedom in pursuing those goods cine needs in life and thus defines social mobility in Igbo society. In this way the Igbo distinguish strongly between the variables of wealth and prestige in awarding values for one's skill and services; important for awarding public honour and recognition among the Igbos.

Similarly, in the status-need model, the Igbo also make further distinctions between the various states of individuals, simply because, for example, he is my father, or a leader, or an elder, or a child, or because he is sick or handicapped. These make perfectly intelligible reasons for determining a fair share, in various circumstances including the distribution of community project and consequently very important for a closely-knit society such as the Igbo. For instance, all humans need to eat, but in times of scarcity women and children are considered first, not because they merit or deserve food, but it is on account of what they are. Thus Furer-Hamendorf is therefore underestimating the approach to the value of merit in traditional societies by asserting that:

---

[57] ibid. p. 165

[58] The phrase "status placement" refers to the generally accepted position an individual occupies in Igbo society. A system of social status in Igbo society implies two major principles of stratification: a common basis of ranking, and a hierarchical order." (cf. V.C. Uchendu, op. c i t. pp. 84-91)

"many primitive societies lack the
idea of merit as a specific aim of
social endeavour. A person's
popularity may be built up in a
casual manner by small acts of
generosity and the demonstration
of more than average qualities of
intellect and heart" [59]

Merit in the concept of social distributive justice is not only important in the struggle for the well-being of the community, but also, with regard to close-knit societies including the Igbo society, it has also institutionalised the quest for social mobility as a way to attend social status and merits.[60]

The Social Distribution Of Burdens

Social distributive justice often concerned itself with deciding between people and therefore is discriminating in its attempt to find appropriate bases for intelligible distribution of goods. Conversely, one would expect justice to employ the same attitude to the social distributions of social burdens.

Burden here is used in a sense of 'mutual responsibility' (duties) shared between members of the community for the buildingor transformation of the community. In this context, to justify the demands made on the members of the community, the Igbo employ the models of wealth-prestige and status-need we have seen as well as the model of equality and impartiality as relevant grounds for the distribution of duties, for every right has a corresponding duty

---

[59] Furez-Hamendorf: Morals and Values, (Weidenfeld, Goldbacks, London, 1969, p. 220)

[60] Ottenberg gave extensive treatment to what he regarded as the three "ethos" for social merits in Igbo society (cf P. Ottenberg "The Afikpo Ibo of Eastern Nigeria" in Peoples of Africa ed. James L. Gibbs, (Holt, Reinehart an Winston, Inc. N.Y. 1965 p. 6.)

attached to it. As we have already seen the other models, we shall concentrate on the model of equality.

The best example to illustrate the distribution of duties in Igbo society is tax collection. In such a case, duties and obligations are shared proportionately on the basis of equality of membership rather than on a differential basis. Justice here ceases to be discriminatory and any judgment of justice which involves a differential treatment has to be justified by "moral considerations of substantial weight"[61]. This is based on the belief that everyone has an inalienable right and the same humanness endowed by God, and intrinsically personality (if not of equal abilities). And for the 19bos, as common agriculturalists, it is assumed that the "automatic" ownership of land provides equal opportunities for individual achievement.

Moreover, the autonomous and segmentary nature of the Igbo socio-political institutions gives Igbo society an equalitarian outlook. Uchendu aptly writes:

> "Equali ty or near equality ensures that
> no one person or group of persons
> acquires too much control over the
> life of others. This is an ideological
> obstacle to the development of a strong
> central authority for the Igbo society"[62]

In practice no human society achieves absolute equality, and the Igbo is no exception. Equality and justice have a relative value and always indicate certain objectivity and appropriateness in Igbo thought. Distinctions always exist in age, sex, and indeed in personhood. For by equality, the Igbo means that which gives to all its citizens an equal opportunity to achieve self-determination, self-expression and self-fulfillment. Consequently, social justice in Igbo society always portrays the relative value of freedom and

---

[61] Sempebwa, op. cit. p. 135
[62] Uchendu, op. cit. p. 19

responsibility in the social setting of the community and thus aims at the welfare of the society. In general, the criteria of relevance adopted by the Igbo in their understanding and application of justice give us a great insight into the moral outlook prevalent in Igbo society, and are thus a good index of the level of moral development attained by it.

CHAPTER FOUR

THE RELEVANCE OF IGBO VALUES OF JUSTICE TO THE CHURCH

In the preceding sections we have discussed the Igbo world-view, the Igbo understanding of man and the nature of social relationship in relation to justice. From such previous discussion, it is obvious that the Igbo concept of justice and its implications in a social context, if carefully evaluated can be relevant to Christianity in Igbo land. As Vatican II rightly specifies the purpose of the Church:

> "To be able to offer all the mysteries
> of salvation and the life brought by
> God, the Church must implant itself
> in all these groups driven by the same
> impulse, which drove Christ through
> his incarnation to bind himself to
> the concrete social and cultural
> conditions of the people among whom
> he lived." (Ad Gentes, 10)

Key points to be noted are the attitude towards life as demanding beneficial reciprocity and sustained through the exercise of justice. There is also the action system sanctioned by religion and thus constituting the 'Omenala' (moral code) which in its operations regulates and prohibits ways of social interactions.[63] It also lays unlimited emphasis on group morality rather than on individual cultivation of goodness itself as a way of ensuring that neither the individual nor the group be deprived of its proper function in the joint realisation of the basic good to which they ar~ committed- namely the fullness of life both in this life and beyond.

It is obvious that the cultivation of this goodness cannot be possible where there is no ethical reflections which guide individuals and ultimately the community in clarifying the logic and adequacy of the values that shaped their lives and experiences.

However, it is worth noting that value as used here means "the quality of a thing which makes it more or less desirable, and useful".[64] Thus, when we ask of the relevance of Igbo value of justice, we are really asking of what significance is justice? In this question one is immediately confronted with the much discussed problem of what attitude should be adopted towards the past and present of justice in Igbo social life in view of what has now become the inevitable interaction between the Christian and Igbo moral values. The question then is: Is the Igbo value of justice of any relevance to Christian ethics?

The Relevance Of Igbo Justice

A careful reflection on the realities underlying Igbo justice reveals remarkable values. Values such as the appeal to God as the upholder of the ideal freedom and life, self-respect, freedom, reciprocal relations of individuals and groups, sharing, mutual responsibility etc. are some of the themes that have occurred again and again in this study.

---

[63] There is some degree of freedom in the effort to achieve one's or group's proper function and this effort is certainly essential to moral responsibility. What is more important than unrestricted freedom is that freedom which allows individuals "to participate in appropriate ways of setting up and directing his relationships and the communities which make demands and set restrictions upon him". (cf. G. Grisez & R. Shaw pp cit. p. 4)

[64] E. llogu, op.cit. p. 119.

Earlier we saw that for the Igbo man, existence always evokes mutual dependence: 'I am •... because we are'. In this context, self-respect and freedom always coincide with the feeling of a firm solidarity between the individual and the groups. There is no question of self-determination of the individual isolated from the group determination. The self-made man is a myth, and a confusing one. Thus in the Igbo society the question of how to be a person is never settled once and for all in any man's life. And it would seem to be the basic Question with which every man is wrestling every day, and all the days of his life.

For the Igbo man, therefore, community or group is a necessity for life and self-determination. This group, as it were, remains present in the isolated individual, keeps an eye on him, encourages or threatens him, demands, in a word, to be consulted and obeyed. It is precisely because the society or community confronted with the same issue of self-determination depends for its existence on the fulfillment of their roles by its individual members. In a sense, therefore, *each* member of the society is dependent on every other member. It is, of course, true that an individual can fail to perform some of the requirements of his role without destroying the social act[65] and thereby, the society. But this is an exception and never the ideal. Thus the importance of *Omenala*, as a moral and legal code and religion cannot be overemphasised. Consequently there is in every community certain minimal level of role fulfillment, varying with the society, which is essential if it is going to continue to be.

Here the basic relationship between social justice and law is that justice like law performs four functions:[66]

i) Justice seeks to establish and maintain certain simple fundamental rules of living together.

ii) Justice provides principles and produces for conflict resolutions between individuals and groups within a society,

---

[65] 'Social Ac t' here is used in the sense of law or social contract.
[66] Cf. E. Kamenka & A. Tay (eds): Justice, (Edward Arnold, London, 1979. pp 4-5)

at least insofar as those individuals and groups accept a version of a common social order that includes submission to law.

iii) To varying degrees at various times and in different places, justice both guarantees and protects existing productive relationships and ways of distributing resources.

iv) It also provides the means for active intervention by the sovereign or state, for whatever reasons, to actualise new principles and policies for resource allocation and to enforce and supervise the carrying out of these in conformity with law.

In this sense the Igbo interpretation of justice and all the ritual avoidance as is evident in the Igbo traditional religion are both relevant and justified insofar as they (Religion and *Omenala)* enable the Igbo to recognise and to ensure the non-violability of the individual rights and claims vis-a-vis the community. Hence Haughey writes:

> "it (social justice) refers to the
> obligations of all citizens to
> aid in the creation of patterns
> of societal organisat.ion and
> activity which are essential both
> for the protection of minimal
> human rights and for the creation
> of mutuality and participation by
> all in social life."[67]

It is significant, however, to note that all moral ideas interpenetrate each, but none is more instructive as justice. Precisely, because justice first and foremost refers to "the other person".

Secondly, justice is always expressed in every society and culture simply despite its complexity. And, above all, it is always seeking to establish the rights and obligations of social relationships and

---

[67] John C. Haughey (ed): The Faith That Does Justice, (Paulist Press, N.Y. 1977, p. 220 cf. also B. Hijring, op. cit. pp. 27-28)

structures without which freedom and self-respect as well as the community would be impossible to come by. Justice is therefore both an idea and an ideal value to which every man strives towards as a moral responsibility for its realisation. In this context it contributes to the building up of community life. It gives meaning to the Igbo sense of sharing and co-operation between members of a family, village or community accidental groups like age-grades and social clubs.

The relevance of Igbo justice can hardly be complete without mentioning the role of religion in Igbo morality. In this case it won't be wrong to assert that religion has enormous influence in the creation of Igbo moral values. Hence in Igbo society "law and custom, tradition, etiquette and religion all are included under the word "*Omenala*". There is no special word for religion".[68] Thus the assertion by Arinze that justice is t he pillar of Igbo morality is an important one because it gives the Igbo an ethico-cultural identity. It gives them a unique way of viewing life-namely life as sacred.

Superficially regarded,[69] all we have seen so far may seem to be a minimally (moral) social relationship-a kind of egoism, one sided and fearful propitiation on the other. But this assessment misses the profound role mutual dependence, God, sharing, reciprocity between all the members of. a group or community and the general duties of justice play in Igbo traditional setting.

The one question to look at now is to what extent is this basic idea of justice Christian?

Justice In Its Proper Perspective: A Lesson And A Task?

Reflecting on what we have seen so far one is left in no doubt about the value of justice in Igbo society. But when it comes 'to the question

---

[68] Arinze, op. cit. p. 30. Cf. E. Njaka, op. cit. p.49

[69] Correia asserts "the Igbo sense of morality is the lowest and most vulgar type of utilitarianism" and this can be misleading. It is obvious that he does not distinguish between principle in belief system and practice in t he social life. (Cf. E. Metuh op. cit. p. 108)

of how much of it is Christian, let alone what attitude should be adopted towards these values, then difficulties arise. Many scholars, philosophers and moralists alike-whatever their orientation-have pointed out this basic aspect of reality, namely every value carries within itself its opposite, at least in the bud. It is accompanied by a counter-value. That is, while we assert the positive goodness of the value of justice, let us not lose sight of its distinctly relative character. Two examples may make it clear.

1. The Idea Of God And His Justice

In Igbo tradition there is a strong sense of the direct and effective influence of Chukwu on man's daily life. The Igbo knows that God is all-powerful, all-knowing, merciful and the final explanation of all, phenomena and that his sense of justice mak.es him to punish the evil and reward the good. He knows that God hates evil and that he always supports those who lack the necessities of life. He is also aware of the existence of non-human spirits including the ancestral spirits and their activities among human beings. They are all interested in human behaviour. More importantly, his whole life is moulded on *Omenala*. He is very conscious of good and evil, just and unjust actions and their consequences in terms of punishment and reward. The emphasis is on the passport to the spirit world and reincarnation.

The consciousness of good and evil, more often than not, makes the Igbo demand and defend his rights. And this would not be possible if he is not aware of them. And to secure his rights he must respect the rights of others, otherwise they will have no respect for him. Enda McDonagh thus notes

> "Relation to the other is a distinctive
> character of justice. It is the function
> of justice to order man his relations
> with his fellows"[70]

---

[70] E. McDonagh, op. cit. p. 155

This respect for other people[71] therefore becomes for the Igbo obligatory and its observance as the basis for reward or punishment, progress or retardment as sanctioned by the gods. Thus life is both a basic good and value to be respected, as found in every culture, though, for the Igbo, it pertains only to those who are identified, by whatever criteria, as belonging to "us", those within the kinship.

The corresponding ethical approach to life is found in Christianity. The Judaeo-Christian religious tradition contains the belief that God is the creator of all things. It also contains the belief that man is made in the image of God, and that man somehow possesses a freedom which resembles the freedom by which God creates. Hence Pius XI insists on this fact that "Belief in God is the one firm foundation of any social order".[9] And such belief, no doubt, is a spiritual force which motivates both the individual and the community to see the respect for one another and respect for life as a moral responsibility in decisions. Most often sin, for example, is not looked upon as primarily an offence against *Chukwu*. It is true in the offender "there is a feeling of guilt and repentance but he fears more the punishment which will unfailingly descend on himself or his relatives or descendants unless he makes the necessary sacrifices. And since *Chukwu* does harm to no one, fear of the spirits and a narrow utilitarianism elbow Him into the background".[72]

But such belief, in practice, does not mean that the idea of God is not clear and outstanding, or that his role in the individual and group relationships is vague. For, it is significant to note, however, that one importance of *Omenala* in Igbo life is that it both embodies the divine commands and provides for the fundamental basis of mutual respect for individual rights in relation to the group. In other words, 'it determines the various levels of social relationships in the group. Hence, *Omenala* is both a social and a moral ideal which calls for a meticulous observation of the social norms for the benefit of both the individual and the group harmonious existence.

---

[71] Pope Paul VI: "Africae Terrarum~ in the Pope Speaks, vol 13, no.1 1968 p. B
[72] 9. Arinze, op cit. p.3l

Therefore, however one may look at the value of justice in Igbo society or whichever attitude one may adopt towards it, it is my view that a new approach is required about how best to impart Christian ideals to the present Igbo society. And for the Christian ethics to be relevant, then the Church cannot overlook their traditional ethico-religious background, particularly the *Omenala'*. No one lives outside space and time; it follows therefore that the idea of God and the value of life will be more meaningful if it is based on all that brings man to God in an atmosphere of justice and freedom as pre-requisites for social order. Therein man will be himself expressing the freedom of the children of God. "The law of the spirit of Christ Jesus has set you free" (Rom. 8:2). Consequently the Igbo Christian morality will be characterised by love, self-control, sacrifice, generosity and courageousness in order to meet the need of all the members of the wider human race.

2. Community Solidarity

The Constitution, the church in the Modern World dwells upon the call to live as a body. Many have welcomed this call regarding this document as recapturing the original Christian idea about community and social justice which will naturally follow from this. This is an outlook familiar to the Igbo. In the Igbo sense of belonging and commitment, the Igbo finds his strength in and from family and community support.

Even before the advent of Christianity in Igboland, religion did influence the entire social life of the individual. But yet, the Igbo sees himself as part and parcel of a group to which he owed existence and protection".[73] The localised group thus defines the community of moral relationship, the setting where principles rather than force prevail. And within these units, social responsibilities generally and responsibilities to one's kin are almost the same thing since nearly all members of the group are related. Lineage duties are one's

---

[73] A. Arinze: The Christian as Citizen, (Archdiocesan Secretariat, Onitsha, Nigeria, 1984, p. 7)

moral duties. In addition to this, however, the respect for one's lineage or group embodied in the attitudes toward traditions and customs *(Omenala)* virtually sums up the dispositions required for harmonious and successful group life in this setting.

As Green, quoting Middleton, observes for the Lugbara:

> "Most of the social interactions of
> any ... individual or family is with
> Kinsmen, and these are essentially
> relations of authority, for which
> there are more formal sanctions. The
> network of authority relations must be
> sustained if Lugbara society is to
> continue and its members to live in
> ami ty and peace"[74]

Thus other traditional values associated with justice, such as generosity, hospitality, respect of elders, co-operation, are not just expressions of justice, or a narrow self-protective measure, (utilitarianism), but also an affirmation of human interdependence.[75] The idea is contained in this proverb: *"Mmadu bu ibe ya"* (Man is his fellow man) and thus corresponds to the social character of the Igbo world-view.

These claims of justice are not known only by the Igbo. They are familiar to the Christian idea of justice. The Igbo principles of justice are even comparable to those Old Testament teaching (cf Ex. 20: 1-17) including the love of neighbours (cf. Deut.6:4 and Lev. 19:18). The norms of justice we have been discussing are not "primarily

---

[74] R. Green. op. cit p. 9

[75] Pope Pius XII: The Rights of Man, (C.T.S. Edition 1943, p. 3). Here the Pope outlined the basis for social life and social peace, noting that "order among intelligent and responsible beings, that is, who pursue an end appropriate t~heir nature-is not a mere extrinsic connection between parts numerically distinct; it tends towards an ever more perfect achievement of internal unity ... grounded in the reality sanctioned by the Creator and by supernatural laws."

derived from a natural philosophical ethic, nor are they of peripheral concern to the Christian Community as an organized institution. There is, in short, a Christian theory of justice and an explicitly Christian obligation to seek this justice, both of which are rooted in the covenant love of God for all persons and in the fulfillment of this love in the death and resurrection of Christ."[76]

By the fact that Christian justice is christocentric and universal brotherhood of human race, the Igbo justice would somehow appear inward and fixated. As in many African cultures, relationships beyond the local group are tense and are filled with moral mistrust or open conflict. Hence forms of conduct such as enmity, quarrelling, theft, unfaithfulness to contracts, which could not be tolerated in the particular group are commended when the act is outside one's lineage. This is where in recent times the societal and communal life in Africa has been misinterpreted and misunderstood by people who think that Africans are the same in their socio-political and cultural identity and therefore calls for a new interpretation of the term "community".

Therefore, the roots of Christocentric justice suggest one final reflection on developing Christian social tradition in Igbo land. And, while recognising the facts of history, culture and language differences, the Church will have no other gospel but that brought about by God through Christ, who demands justice, truth, love and fellowship of the whole human race. The justice of God knows no boundaries of tribe or region. Thus the essence of the social character of the universe is the call of man to the universal "brotherhood".

In other words, the view expressed in *Gaudium et Spes*, of the possibility of achieving mutuality and reciprocal interdependence in society clearly calls for significant changes in both individual behaviour and institutional arrangements. Solidarity and concern for one's kin are also moral responsibilities to those beyond one's immediate group.

This is what the Bishops of the 1972 Synod meant when they said:

---

[76] J.C. Haughey, op. cit. p. 226 f.

"Action on behalf of justice and participation
in the transformation of the world fully
appear to us as a constitutive dimension
of the preaching of the gospel, or, in
other words, of the Church's mission for
redemption of the human race and its 14
liberation from every oppressive situation."[77]

---

[77] Marie Gibbin: "Reflections on Experience in the Village Apostolate", <u>Afer</u>, vol.
18, 1976, p. 148

GENERAL CONCLUSION

The significance of the word "relevance" in this study is to indicate that whatever is the Igbo traditional value of justice, in its inspriation, orientation and content, it could be a basis for the better understanding of the Igbo moral values in general and their ethical attitudes in particular. I very much acknowledge and I hope many would agree that the study of ethical systems is very much in its infancy and thus it calls for further investigations into Igbo moral values. Consequently, such research would lead to a better understanding of the Igbo man. (Cf. *Lumen Gentium,* 16).

I quite recognise other possible areas one would have under normal circumstances treated in detail for a better understanding of the Igbo traditional value of justice. But given space and time, I have tried to reconstruct as far as possible the Igbo notions of justice as well as its applications in daily life, confining myself only to the traditional society rather than with the modern. We only hope it would have relevance to the way non-Igbos approach the needs and experiences of the Igbo people in their ever changing world.[78]

In dealing with justice in Igbo society, one is once again confronted with the many-sidedness of justice through which the meaning of justice continues to elude human mind. Maguire beautifully points

---

[78] It is significant to note that the rapid transformation of Igbo traditional society t~hat it is today is largely due to the fact that the Igbo culture is as "particularistic as it is universalistic" That is, change is the bulwark of Igbo culture. (cf. Njaka, op. cit pp 51-53 esp. S. Ottenberg: "Ibo Receptivity to Change" in Continuity and change in African Cultures, ed W.B. Bascom and J.M. Heiskovitz (Univ. Press, Chicago 1958, pp 130-143)

out that "implicit in any conception of justice are assumptions about the nature of personhood and the rapport between the individual and society."[79]

All that one can say is that notions of justice in Africa have a unique dimension. And when it is referred to an agrarian community with well-knit brotherly social units, justice would appear as a process of recognition, articulation, and selection imposed on man by the necessities of life. Social adjustments are therefore not only necessary, but also are all critical parts of the maturation and refinement of human society brought about by the appeal to justice as an end to the persistent injustice in human society. Thus there is no doubt that issues of justice are as old as history and that in various times and in different circumstances men have always felt the need for a "totality of social harmony" for the meaningfulness of human existence.

---

[79] H.D. Maguire, op. cit. p. 76

❧ ❧ ❧

BIBLIOGRAPHY

ABBOT, W.M. (ed)   The Documents of Vatian II
                     Corpus Books, N.Y. 1966)

ACHEBE, C.   Things Fall Apart
                     (Heinemann Press, London, 1958)

AMADI, E.   Ethics in Nigerian Culture
                     (Heinemann Press, Ibadan 1982)

ARINZE, F. A.   Sacrifice in Igbo Religion
                     (Univ. Press, Ibadan, Nigeria, 1970)
                     The Chritian As Citizen
                     (Archdiocesan Secretariat, Onitsha,
                     Nigeria 1984)

BASDEN, G.T.   Niger Ibos
                     (Frank Cass, London, 1966)

BERSON, H   The Two Sources of Morality and
                     Religion (Doubleday & Co. N.Y.,
                     1935)

CAMPBELL, T.   Seven Theories of Human Society
                     (Clarendon Press, London, 1981)

CHUKWUMA, H.O.   Oral Tradition of the Ibos
                     (An unpublished Ph.D thesis in
                     Philosophy, Univ. of Birmingham
                     1974)

DINE, G.U.   Traditional Leadership as Service
                     Among the 1gbo of Nigeria,

	(Pontifical Univ. Laternense, Rome, 1983)
EWIN, R.E.	<u>Co-operation and Human Values</u> (The harvester Press, London, 1981)
FORDE, D. & JONES, G.I.	<u>The Ibo and Ibibio-Speaking Peoples of South-Eastern Nigeria</u> (International African Institute, London, 1962)
FORDE, D.	"Justice and Judgment Among the Southern Ibo Under Colonial Rule" in <u>African Law</u>: <u>Adaptation and Development,</u> (eds).Kuper, H. at Kuper L. (Univ. of Calif. Press, Berkeley, and Los Angeles, 1965, pp. 79-96
FUCHS, J	<u>Human Values and Christian Morality</u> (Gill and Macmillan, Dublin, 1977 (impression)
FURER-HAIMENDORF, C.	<u>Morals and Merit,</u> (Weidenfeld Goldbacks, London, 1969
GIBLIN, M :	"Reflections on Experience in the Village Apostolate", Ater, vol. 18, 1976, pp 145-1')
GINSBERG, M.	<u>On Justice In Society.</u> (Penguin Books, London, 1965)
GRISEZ, G. & SHAW, R.	<u>Beyond the New Responsibility,</u> (Univ. of Notre Dame, Notre Dame, 1974)
HARING, B.	<u>The Law of Christ Vol III</u> Mercier Press, Dublin 1963)
HATCH, E.	<u>Culture and Morality,</u> (Columba Univ. Press, N.Y. 1983)

HAUGHEY, J.C. (ed)	The Faith that does Justice, (Paulist Press, N.Y. 1977)
HORTON, W.R.G.	"God, Man and the Land in a Northern Ibo Vi llage-group" Africa, Vol. XXVI, No.1 (1956) pp.17-28 "The Ohu System of Slavery in a Northern Ibo Village-group, Africa, Vol. XXIV, No.4 (1954) pp 311-335
ILOANUSU, O.	Myths of the Creation of Man and the Origin of Death in Africa, (European Univ. Studies, Frankfurt am Main, 1984)
ILOGU, E.	Christianity and Igbo Culture, (Nok publ. London, 1974)
KAMENKA, E. and TAY, A.E. (eds)	Justice (Edward Arnold, London, 1979,
KELBLEY, G. (ed)	The Value of Justice, (Fordham Univ. Press, N.Y. 1979)
KUDADJIE, J.N.	"Does Religion Determine Morality in African Societies? A View Point", in Religion in a Pluralistic Society, Leiden, 1976, pp . 60-77
LEIS, P. E.	Inculturation and Socialisation In An Ijaw Village, (Holt, Rinehart and Winston, N.Y. 1972)
LIEBER, J.W.	Ibo Village Communities (Univ . of Ibadan, Nigeria, 1971)
LE VINE, R.A	Dreams and Deeds - Achievement Motivation in Nigeria (Univ. Press, Chicago, 1965)
LUCAS, J.R.	On Justice Clarendon Press, London, 1980)

MAYS, LL.	"Justice : Perspective from the Prophetic Tradition," <u>Interpretation,</u> Vol. 37, 1983 pp 5 - 17
MAYER, A.C. (ed)	<u>Culture and Morality</u> (Oxford Univ. Press, Delhi 1981)
MBITI, J.S.	<u>Concepts of God in Africa,</u> (Heinemann Press, London, 1970) <u>African Religions and Philosophy</u>, (Heinemann Press, London 1969)
McDONAGH, D.C.	<u>The Demands of Simple Justice,</u> (Gill and Macmillan, Dublin 1980)
- ed)	<u>Moral Theology Renewed,</u> (Gill and son, Dublin 1965)
MEEK, C.K.	<u>Law and Authority in a Nigerian Tribe</u> (Oxford Univ . Press, London, 1937)
MELDEN, A.I.	<u>Rights and Persons</u> (Basil Blackwell, London, 1977)
METUH, E.	<u>God and Man in African Religion,</u> (Geoffrey Chapman, London, 1981)
NEW CATHOLIC ENCYCLOPEDIA	Vol. VIII (McGraw-Hill Books, London & N. Y. 1967)
NJAKA, E.N.	<u>Igbo Political Culture</u> (North western Univ. Press, Evanston, 1974)
O'DONNELL, W.E.	"Religion and Morality Among the Ibo of Southern Nigeria" <u>Primitive Man,</u> 44 (193l), pp . 54-6u
OGBALU, F.C.	<u>Ilu Igbo</u> {The Book of Igbo Proverbs (Univ. Press, Nigeria, 1965)
OGLETREE, T.W.	<u>The Use of Bible in Christian Ethics,</u> (Fortress Press, Philadelphia, 1983)

OTTENBERG, S.	"Improvement Associations Among the Afikpo lbo," <u>Africa,</u> Vol XXV, No.1 (1955) pp. 1-27
	"The Afikpo Ibo of Eastern Nigeria", in <u>Peoples of Africa,</u> ed Gibbs, J.L. Holt, Rinehart & Winston, N.Y. 1965)
	"Ibo Receptivity to Change", in <u>Continuity and change in African Cultures</u> ed. Bascom, W.B. and Herskovits, J.M. (Univ. Press, Chicago, 1958)
POBEE, J .5. (ed)	<u>Religion, Morality and Population Dynamics,</u> (Univ. of Ghana, Legon, 1977)
POPE PIUS XII	<u>The Rights of Man</u> C.T.S. Edition 1943)
	<u>Quadragesimo Anno</u> (C.T.S . Edition, 1931)
POPE PAUL VI	<u>Africae Terrarum</u> The Pope Speaks,Vol 13, No.1, 1968)
POPE JOHN XXIII	<u>Pacem in Terris</u> (C.T.S. edition 1963)
	<u>Mater et Magistra</u> (C.T.S. edition 1961)
POPE LEO XI II	<u>Rerum Novarum</u> (C.T.S. edition 1891)
POPE JOHN PAUL II	<u>Justice and Peace</u> (C.T . S. edition)
RAMSEY., I. T.	<u>Christian Ethics and Contemporary Philosophy</u> (S.C.M. Press, London, 1966)

RADCLIFFE-
BROWN, A.R.   <u>Structure and Function in Primitive
                               Society</u> (Cohen and West Ltd.
                               London 1952)

RAY, B.C.   African Religion: Symbol, Ritual
                               and Community
                               (Prentice-Hall, Inc. Englewood
                               Clipps, New Jersey, 1965)

REDFIELD, R.   <u>The Primitive World and Its
                               Transformations</u>
                               (Cornell Univ. Press, N.Y. 1953)

RUCH, E.A. and   <u>African Philosophy</u>
ANYANWU, K.C .   (Catholic Book Agency, Rome 1981)

SEMPEBWA , J.W.   <u>African Traditional Moral
                               Norms and Their Implications
                               for Christianity</u> (The Steyl Press,
                               Netherlands, 1983)

SHORTER, A.   <u>African Culture and the Christian
                               Church</u> (S.C.M . Press, London,
                               1973)

TALBOT, P. A.   <u>Life in Southern Nigeria</u>
                               Frank Cass, London, 1967)

TAYLOR, V.J.   <u>The Primal Vision</u>
                               (S.C.M. Press, London, 1969)

TEMPLES, P.   <u>Bantu Philosophy</u>
                               (Presence Africaine (English
                               Edition) Paris, 1953)

The Ethics of Aritotle: (Trans. Thomson, J . A.K. Penguin
Nicomacheu Ethics   Books, Baltimore, 1953)

UCHENDU, V.C.   The Igbo of South-East Nigeria
                               (Holt, Rinehart and Winston , N.Y.
                               1965)

UMEASIEGBU, R.N.   <u>The Way We Lived</u>
                               (Heinemann, Ibadan, 1969)

USANGA, B.D.   <u>The Church in the Era of Cultural
                      Revival</u> (St. Therese's Press, Calabar,
                      Nigeria)

UZUKWU, E.E.   "Igbo Spirituality"
                      <u>L'Afrique Et Les formes De Vie
                      Spirituelle</u> Vol. 17, Nos. 33-34 (1981)
                      pp 155 - 172

WALL, G.B.   "Primitive Cultures and Ethical
                      Universalslt <u>International
                      Philosophical Quarterly</u>
                      Vol VII, 1967, pp 470 - 482

WESTERMANN, D.   <u>Africa and Christianity</u>
                      (Oxford Univ. Press, London, 1937)

WINTER, G.   <u>Social Ethics</u> (SCM Press, London,
                      1968

Printed in the United States
By Bookmasters